BLACKBERRY WINTER

Poems
by
Helga Kidder

BLUE LIGHT PRESS ❖ 1ST WORLD PUBLISHING

1ST WORLD
PUBLISHING

SAN FRANCISCO ❖ FAIRFIELD ❖ DELHI

BLACKBERRY WINTER

Copyright ©2016 by Helga Kidder

1ST WORLD LIBRARY
PO Box 2211
Fairfield, Iowa 52556
www.1stworldpublishing.com

BLUE LIGHT PRESS
www.bluelightpress.com
Email: bluelightpress@aol.com

BOOK & COVER DESIGN
Melanie Gendron

COVER ART
Google — Images

AUTHOR PHOTO
Everett Kidder

FIRST EDITION

Library of Congress Control Number: 2015959454

ISBN 9781421837468

—for Everett, Lauren, Galen, and Gerlinde
and all visual artists who inspire poetry

CONTENTS

I.

II.

III.

IV.

I.

*" then she pours her hair
into the mirror, and . . .
drinks quietly from her image."*

—Rainer Maria Rilke *"Lady at a Mirror"*

House Cleaning

Spring stirs a tangle of underbrush,
tiny sprouts of chokeberry coaxed by sun.
The year's waltz,
wind and sun leading the days.
Birds whittle their flutes,
crosshatch nests.
I thin out closets, brown-bag stilettos and flats
for Goodwill, snap begonias and geraniums
to stubs for beginnings.

I thought winter was a gentle hand
strobing night's soft sheen of stars.
I thought frost was a cleansing rain
looping around branches of magnolia,
brushing the blue and white painted house.
The house is a river I love
to sit by, searching the bottom for shards,
shimmering coins of light
I bank like wishes
between heaven and earth.

The Helga Paintings

—by Andrew Wyeth

I'm not the woman in the painting.
My hair is not red.
I don't have her Nordic cheekbones
or her impassive Nordic manner.
I don't break a man's heart.

Some nights I water limp ivy trailing the wall,
sweep dust balls with a horsehair broom.
Some nights I brush time
past each rounded shoulder, watch how
the mirror looks into my eyes.
Tomorrow, I could outshine the sun.

Genealogy of the Planet

I am earth's dark loam
layering herself for seeds.

I am the iris' corm, pushing blades
to her fleur-de-lis, the sugar maple's sap,
unguent veining trunk and branches.

I am the lizard's slivering shimmer,
the swallowtail's fiery wings
swirling the air.

I am the clouds, the wind, the rain
sweeping dust off roofs and treetops,
the sun's rays coaxing saplings.

I am the moon and the stars
rotating their night lights.

I am the universe
pulsing, stretching arms wide,
exhaling . . .

I am creation.

Purification

Rain scrubs the blue house,
pummels the kitchen window.

I slip feet into orange rain boots,
tell our dog, *you need a bath.*
Let's walk to the mailbox.

He doesn't know rain
is water, the same force
he fights in the tub.

Rain spills all it knows
onto trees, shrubs, bulbs
waking from sleep,
transcending inner lives.

In dreams I jump hurdles of fear,
open my heart's red purse
for secrets never told.

Ground swallows rain.
Rain shows us the way.

Revelation

The mind wings daily
through DNA,
a double helix constructed
eons ago
when the map of the world
was first drawn,
then rolled into cells,
thread-like or disc-shaped,
where God's hand spins
like a *dreidel*.

City Garden

Door aslant, path
narrowed by overgrown
slouching shrubs,
mornings
when I don't want to get dressed.

An apricot tree spreads
limbs studded with fruit buds.
Each branch suspends tinsel
that glitters
like angels' hair falling.

A bicycle tackles a bush.
A head board slants a windowless shed.
Metal chairs and tables, a couch
invite to lounge with a drink in hand –
forget that snakes could hide
in knee-high grass.

How the Garden of Eden has changed
after the serpent minced words.
Every object attacks my thoughts,
either to accept what I have seen
or to reason out its existence,
like the piano presiding
over this odd assembly,
lid open to play.
DON'T.

The House Trembles

". . . how far does my life reach
and where does the night begin" —Rilke

Pacing in front of the sliding glass door,
our dog barks at the night's storm.

Thor's wagon rumbles across the sky again.
His spear of light bares my bed of dreams:

I drink from the river that flows
along the arc of my soul. At its banks,
I stand underneath wild cherry blooms
hanging like new-born stars.

You swing the mattock into earth,
weed crown vetch crowding roots.

Together, we plant a yellow rose
for thirty-four years of married love,
encourage it to climb
the arbor.

I wake to the crackle, crack, and thump
of a branch falling on the forest floor.

Thunder and lightning chase clouds to dawn.
The dog sighs, settles on his pillow.

How far inside does the river of light reach?
Where does night begin?

The Three Ages of Women

—by Gustav Klimt

After love possessed her womb,
a young woman holds her suckled girl
against her breasts' fullness.
An olive branch drapes her hips.
Days of gold and purple
gild their early years.

Behind them, the shadow of a woman,
skin yellowed and paper-thin,
legs, arms blue-veined,
shoulders hunched forward like barriers,
belly bloated with age
below her pendulous breasts.
She covers her eyes with one hand,
youth's rainbow gone,
darkness a guide to the underworld.

I believe Klimt
forgot to paint one more woman.
She transcends the body.
Her crown, a shock of wisdom.
Face furrowed by years of worry
wrinkling a smile.
She knows the words of her heart,
the flames of opinion,
her season's simmering fire.

Insomnia

Moonlight branches the window,
sprays my mouth with notes and syllables
bursting into words.
Trees yawn the rhythm of cicadas
waking after 17 years, ready to party.
Nerves strung like a violin.

The house sleeps.
Books on the shelf dream of their heroes.
They lean into each other like passengers
cozied into a train's compartment
as it rolls rhythmically
on rails running from coast to coast.

Caught in the middle of night
like Jonah inside the whale,
I listen to the body's organ music,
reverberating through its bony vault,
wonder when darkness will open her mouth.

Night Flight

Night backs into day
as if you had spoken magic words,
commanding the two to separate.

In darkness we danced
with wind and clouds.

You stashed words into my pocket of silence,
sparked the light I carry inside.

Thoughts embroider memory—
the town we left,
the river's dark claim of lives,
the daily revelation of light
clinging to white-washed stone houses.
Rooms filled with echoes.

Woman with Folded Arms

We can guess why Picasso painted
melancholy into the woman's
gaunt face, her slumped shoulders.

Hair pushed under a dark cap,
she stares into the blue space
of middle age.

Arms crossed beneath her
languid breasts as if to lessen
the pit in her stomach.

He said he found
a younger model, that today
would be their last session.

She sits quietly. No tears
escape her averted eyes.
No sniffles into a handkerchief.

She knew womanhood
would bring her
to this day.

He dips his brush
into a darker blue to finish
quickly, eyes on tomorrow.

Follow the ribbon of twilight

"Mermaid Initiation" —Diane Frank

The sun straddles the day
thinking of the moon's coolness
last night, shining one half of itself
over the meadow where love grows
like wildflowers, their soft blue
and buttery yellow blooms painting
our hands.

What is love, anyway?
A cello's bow gleaning melody from strings?
A butterfly
stunned at the flower's sweetness.
Did she forget she can fly?

The past pushes the door,
then turning away,
letting it flap in aftermath.

Matsushima by Korin

  —Ink painting on a six-panel paper screen

Ocher turbulence like flames
of passion
time has turned muddy yellow.

Mountains scale a swelling sea,
meet the sky in clouds,
rolling like waves.
We would have capsized,
swept away by undercurrents.

Korin's ink hatted mountain tops
with scrub pine,
parried white-capped waves
and clouds, like our arguments.

As wind, water and mountains ripple
moonlight over paper,
the heart rises and falls,
renews in mist.

This Is The Hour I Like Best

>—Countess Olenska to Archer in *The Age of Innocence*

The hour when we are our own planets,
our passions like haloed moons,
fiery stars, where hearts float
in the sky and open
their wide umbrellas to save us.

The hour when we think
if we lean back a second's tick
or swivel our feet against time,
we can avoid the wrong step.

This is the hour I like best:
When the world's snarl and bite
sits obediently at my feet,
and the hour licks the hem of time.

Monet's *Waterlilies*

Most days I am a pond
behind the house, romancing
roving clouds, bending
waterlilies toward noon
as cattails weave the hours.

But share my look:
This pond's dark brush strokes reach
deep into a universe of stars
while the foreground falls
into the frame's rectangle.

Isn't it easy to fall
into the self
if unprepared for the expected.

Monet burned thirty studies
of this pond, *and this one, too,*
he said, *should be destroyed.*

The Scar

I will stitch your face like a loved one's,
eclipsing the hole,
mending skin without puckering

said the surgeon. With the tipped angle
of a scalpel, he excised and culled
the floweret budding skin.

The scar centers your cheek
so your smile stops underneath the eye,
funnels into a wrinkle,
a permanent frown of whiffing sulfur.

In dreams the scar is a bluebird's
air-filled bone taking flight,
feathering the sky.

At waking your hand strokes
the fallen nestling
that hovers, shivering.

After Knee Surgery

> *". . . to go through the undone*
> *burdened and as if bound . . ."*
> —Rilke, "The Swan"

Awkward on land,
I glide into a pool of water.

My mind flutters
past laurel to rose,

hovers, and plucks
memory's plume.

Mother on her knees
scouring, waxing, polishing circles
into someone else's parquet.

She never spoke poetry
but knew perseverance:

Lifting her body for flight.

Blackberry Winter

Blessing or curse —
living in the sun, the moon,
the moment of the day,
like the *Piraha* tribe —
past smashed blank
against memory's wall.

Only the immediate counts —
a water kettle boiling,
lifted off the fire

or blackberry limbs hooked
into yours, lashing the skin,
tomorrow's scars seen
as *the way it has always been.*

No memory of your younger sister,
bike brake failing downhill,
crashing into a cement wall,

basket of blackberries spilling,
tiny beehives bursting,
seeping red into dust
beside her broken body.

Your memory, a hummingbird
sipping devil's brush blooms,
hoping for sustenance
in a blaze of flames.

Roots

As if standing in your laundry kitchen,
forest fog steams to the cloud ceiling.

Rain ruled the week like a dictator,
roused bed straw,
leaved the forest green
except one oak
tilting toward the house.

Time withdrew breath when you said,
I wonder how it feels. I've never died before.

Disease festered and gripped your body,
shutting down one organ at a time.
The nightmare of slow death.

After you leave this world,
will roots continue to listen to wisdom
sweetgum and sugar maple whisper?

Song

Though I never heard her singing,
I hear mother's song tonight—
icy, white wind blustering
through maple and sourwood,
herding leaves into drifts.

Born into farm life, she overcame fear
early, forced to crawl under a cow's belly
at her older brother's command.
Hair full and brown as a handful of chestnuts.

A tiny crack in the wall,
face stoic in chaos,
war and divorce,
fissures as tectonic plates shift,
settle on top of each other.
Hair reduced to salt and pepper.

The two burner wood stove witness
to her mastery, blending spinach with onions,
potatoes, butter, and nutmeg.
My sister and I fought for seconds.

As wrens and chickadees hopped
through the garden, she smiled, remembering:
are you not worth much more than they?*
Hair silver strands of the moon.

The moon a magician tonight
weaving through branches
the spell of her song.
Now you hear it.
Now you don't.

*Matt. 6:26

II.

"So let us love
confident as is the light
in its struggle with darkness"

—William Carlos Williams *"Asphodel, That Greeny Flower"*

What Water Says

I.

Silver tongue seeking the self,
                          the clear sound of water
washes, curves my body.
                          Breaths deep and controlled,

memory curls around my arms, hands,
                                    expands.

A purple finch in Fedora soaks in the bird bath.

Dahlias lap morning dew.

II.

I began listening
              to the river's voice,
                                its undercurrent —
return to the sea
    your ancient home.

Flirting with the water's edge,
                          I dipped my spoon,
emptied it in long sweeps,
      fell in love with the water's face.

Light stuttered over ripples as I followed the call.

III.

I hear the translation, the words,
      *rivers of living water**
flowing inside me,
    shutter temptation

that clings to shore grass,
      reminisces in the red bird's dirge.
Twilight hangs
   like a leaf by its fragile stem
       as night elbows
the day off the world's table.

*John 7:38

When I Let the River Answer

Each ripple is a second gone.
I want to hold back the flow,
yet gooseflowers and clover nudge my feet.

The frogs' high whines lament rhapsody.

Cottonwood catkins float
like river fairies
to midday siesta.

Husbands nap next to their wives.

Your answer is balm.
I quiver next to blades of grass.

Oleander

Leashed to pottery, petunias
brush the brick wall,
long-legged lilies offer dawn in orange bowls,
and maidengrass bows to the garden's curve.

They don't understand the clock ticking,
time hanging on house siding.
They only know seasons drifting days
like homeless wanderers.

Eyes painted on wings,
a peacock butterfly senses nectar
sweetening oleander clusters,
not toxins cruising lance-shaped leaves.

Memory nestles on an evening bench
sipping iced champagne with you,
oleander's red perfume
stunning the heart.

Snow White in the Twenty-first Century

Resting in her glass coffin,
she appeared alive,
ivory snow,
ruby blood,
hair dark as a starless night
draping over her shoulders.

Love at first glance,
the wandering prince claimed her
like a relic for his castle.

Seven is a godly number:
transformed dwarves, lights,
beds, knives, forks, spoons,
and plates into goodness
that could not be denied.

Good things come in threes,
though owl, crow, and dove mourned.
No binding, no poisoned comb or apple
could take Snow White's life.

Her savior, the prince,
and his helpers
carrying the glass coffin,
stumbled on rocky terrain,
loosening the poisoned apple —
stepmother's pride.
The prince offered Snow White
marriage as salvation.

So good triumphed over evil
as they celebrated their vows,
put red-hot iron boots
on the stepmother's feet
for her final dance.

Never is the mirror blamed
for jealousy and pride,
but nothing is
what appears to be.

The Cellist

—Rebecca Merblum's concert with Placedo Domingo

Bow hand rolling across strings,
she listens to the wings of her inner ear,
shells that form in layers and open.

She meets the strings like a dancer
in georgette, limber and graceful,
delivers sound deep in wood
as the melody colors the concert hall.

Placedo spins her into pirouettes,
lifts and throws her into air,
coaxes her low to the ground.

She glides through the field of notes
with eyes closed,
as with a first kiss.

Horn of Plenty

I climb from frigid water,
think of you
who cemented my time
to this world:

a fading speck on a Painted Lady's wing,
a black gum branch loosening,
the rainbow of grace.

You are my angel of the lyre,
eyes centered on my soul's
leaping flames.

I take my light from you
one heart leaf at a time,
before I slowly crumble
into the wall of darkness,

where you wait
in history's stacked stones.

Eau de Toilette

A spray of citrus, lemon yellow
puckering my mouth,
the scent of mother's boiled quince
dripping through cloth for jelly
or her waxed and shined parquet floor.
Your handkerchief unfolding,
wiping my eyes at your proposal.

When Klimt painted Malcesine at Lake Garda
below lemon groves, each brush stroke
carried the aroma into rose gardens,
through fields of poppies and marguerites,
white-washed houses, opened windows.

Is it your kiss feathering my tongue,
goldenrod brushing the wind's canvas,
or Klimt's love for limoncello?

An ocher ring haloes the moon
on cold, starless nights.
Your body pressed into mine,
promises sliced paper-thin.

Study of a New Medium

Afternoon pollution thickens the river's bend.
Heat contorts weeds below.

Inside, patience stretches impatience.
The table has no clock.
I need to forget what time it is.

A painter sometimes obliterates what displeases
the eye. El Greco elongated his images
as if to trick them into a sadness,
the body's let-down.

I need to expand, unlike Picasso,
this corner of an afternoon from a room
into a river I forged in childhood
to cover my feelings.

I want to paint your body like Monet
at different hours of the night
into a harsher, yellow light.

So much depends on the mind.
If I am lucky, it will rain
all over Tennessee tonight.

The Lute Player

—by Caravaggio

He also plays the viola,
instrument and bow resting on the table,
but now his slender hands pluck the lute
like heart strings.

White robe virginal, dark locks
seducing his face,
his eyes drawn beyond the painting's edge.
His *amore mio* must have entered
through a hidden door. He quavers
one of the pensive melodies
popular in 1595 Italy.

Two white orchids, a crimson rose,
wildflowers in a vase
next to pears, lime, and *melanzane*
scent his song floating in air,
rapping on her heart's transom.

Witness to this private recital,
take a look into his soul:
He does not check his music sheet.
He knows the words, the strings by heart.
He also knows the magic of silence
afterwards.

Madame Brune's Garden

Ronsard roses, named for the poet,
the size of my face.
Marguerites daisy a corner
and irises march the path's curve blue.

You answer my, *tres magnifique,*
with a swell of French I can't follow.

Lavender and fuchsia leaf the perimeter,
wait for summer's burst,
the scent of *violette.*

Spring light sprays the lawn,
illumines our sentiments,
that creation is alive in a garden,

a bridge between languages,
a dove chanting
to the flow of the river.

Strasbourg Cathedral — France

It took four hundred years to complete.
We nod, peruse stained glass windows,
life-sized saints domesticating aisles,
trace a finely carved sandstone vine
climbing twenty steps to the chancellery.

Each day the sculptor returned to etch
another curve, another curling tendril,
a new leaf above a grape cluster.
Did he dream fingering vines at night?

The vine grew like his longing to finish
as he chiseled, sculpted, exposed
each turn like a parable preached,
looked back astonished on his entire life.

Pigeon Houses

In my dream a pigeon flies
through miniature castle towers,
stacked stone, flapping
for a way out.

I skim tall wheat fields
or fiery poppies,
a chorus of grapevines humming
sun and rain into round fruit.

Prized as a girl's dowry,
messenger of secret notes tied to my leg,
thighs a tender delicatessen,
I am unsettled like a coin
flipped for possession.

I want to escape these hot flares
folding inward,
wish for tinier wings
on their journey through the pocketful
of days left to spend.

Flames exhausted to a flicker,
I die to the dream
at the end of myself
as morning
ruffles the tips of my feathers.

The Muse of Malta

Calypso still sits on white cliffs
above the *Mediterranean*,
gathers her sheer blue sheath,
unbraids her hair
fluttering in brisk morning wind.

She is muse to your small boat of wisdom,
tossed high by white-bearded waves
that hem you in.

You are unsure of her pose on calcium rocks.
Is she guarding old lovers
like pock-marked stones
while she wills the sea and your wavering boat
closer to her shore?

Like Odysseus, you climb the steep rocks
eager for her words,
coming swiftly now,
as waves below rise, crest, fall away.

Painted Grace

—for Lisa Seago —Just Beyond

Salt of the earth,
if it weren't for the clouds,
your painting would calm the spirit,
would allow the boat
of my mind to rustle stormless
through the marsh
before ebb returns to the Atlantic.

Clouds fill the sky
like bundles of soiled linen
above cord grass, rush, and sedge.
Roots below, tightly intertwined,
shelter muskrat, frog, turtle.

The coming and going
of life: single cell flutters,
proteins chaining together
are daily miracle,
a hidden city of tenants,
scurrying, slithering,
swapping microscopic swarms.

Gray-tinged clouds grumble
on the verge of releasing rain,
as when someone is asked to share
abundance,
and does.

Horizon darkened to murky green,
the first drops fall just beyond
your painting, cool built-up heat
before the tide returns again,
seasons the marsh with salt.

Tennis in Yorkshire

for Sue B.

Facing the North Sea,
        sun veneers its final glow
                over the lawn.

Ladies in white dress
        shuffle and glide,
                racket yellow balls over nets.

Victorian houses court one side
        like cheerleaders
                in lacework and fringe.

Balls barely bounce.
        Players bend knees deep,
                propel returns.

Gulls wing the horizon.
        Narrow beach houses offer
                a spot of tea inside.

A herd of clouds grazes the sky.
        Doves garoo to their young.
                Deuce, tiebreak, overhead smash.

Shadows slice courts in half.
        Evening fog chills the shore.
                Final score: Up in air.

Memorial Day

New York is all about bikes.
Skinny bikes, fast bikes,
high end bikes,
get-you-there-quick bikes,
no-gas, no-oil-change bikes.

I stroll Brooklyn's Fifth Avenue,
weave through narrow shops,
finger livelihoods of artists —

a white bike leaning into the street sign,
flower garland blooming
handlebars, frame.

This is Liza Padilla's memorial,
visual artist caught in a maze
of talent, tangled
in traffic, white-washed.

Celebrating Your Life

for Gene and Billie

Birds bicker through the open screen door,
day bright and fresh in the face.

The newspaper says, 84 today.

I sip a cup of dark brew, watch this fiery ball stride
passage of time across the sky.

I want to return to sender an entire year,
retrieve the days
before you said, *finished.*

Why do I chase the past like a thief?

Helios and his horses
won't give back the days
before I would wake alone.

Bless this dark, bitter drink
your passing poured into me.

I will watch you dance with the stars tonight.

Hartsfield Airport, Atlanta

I forage faces for clues
as they spill languages birthed
at the tower of Babel,
eager to find a connection.

Endless lines, sorted like lentils
on the kitchen table, disperse
for deeper inspection,
free will lugged like baggage.

I am one of few in limbo
or what some call purgatory,
suffering silently for redemption,
watching others inch forward
to the next level of judgment,

wonder if the stain of cheap words between us
will turn to gold,
if the shards love left behind
will be rediscovered like new galaxies,
farther away in distance and time.

Sun tints tarmac
black and white beside silver wings.
I shoulder an over-sized bag's tenacity,
confess the life my face wears.

Anniversary

When I was a swan, long-necked,
body pure as snow's first fall,
my whistles feathered shore grass,
raised your wings and sounded your trumpet.

We framed our nest on solid ground,
cultivated off-spring like flowers after rain,
but forgot to dazzle each other's eyes.

Earth shifted,
the bed rocked, garbled vows.
Years buckled and peeled off like paint.

Blue bird, purple finch, yellow warbler
flit through our dream feeders,
spill seeds sprouting golden suns.
We've molded ourselves to a settled house,
bowed to age one bone at a time.

Mated for life,
you sweep dirt tracked inside with broom and pan.
I bind weeds and wild flowers
into a life-sized wreath.

Street Arabs in Sleeping Quarters at Night

photograph by Jacob A. Riis

Scattered like seeds on a house stoop,
three boys lie asleep,
legs angled into bodies,
arms propping heads against stone.
Their father collapsed on the house bench,
head leaning into clapboard
as if watching over them in sleep.
They've exhausted the day.

Did they scrape fields and sheds
for the next meal,
instead chewed leaves,
a fistful of dirt?

They pleaded for what was not given,
door shut.
Always someone refusing to share.

What measure of will
decided their fate?

Tongues swollen and sore,
blessed sleep lead them
to corn and wheat fields,
bursting.

Crop Circles

What could gods learn from us?
That we crave more god-like moments than they?

The day a maze,
we stake the center, get dizzy circling,
unable to pin-point what waits at sundown.

Hours like wheat standing too high
to see signs for detours or a wash-out.

Moments like blades of grass
weaving the breeze
a careless touch cuts to blood.

Your arms enfolding me from behind
you kissed the hairline of my neck,
then walked away.

Do gods bother with the details of human life,
break moments into Euclidian geometry?
Not melody?

Moments they fling back into the universe,
invisible and weightless.

Olive Orchard, Greece

Scorched by the summer sun, grass
in this black and white photo
is blanched, as if after disaster.

A make-shift ladder leans haphazard
against the knee of an olive tree.
I don't know what the lens didn't capture.

Perhaps bare olive trees and bird-free air
signify that nothing was left to glean,
that a whirlwind lifted all to the clouds.

More than 2000 years old, these olive trees
have witnessed history, fulfilling time,
asking, *how long?*

After Ten Years

for my best friend's son

Rain washes the window
like wet skin, morning
hiking over Stringer's Ridge.

You write, *Nothing*
changes here
except the sun
as it sidles across the prison yard,
scales the wall
on its journey to the horizon.

Head shaved, you teach Tai-Chi
to fellow inmates, loosen
muscles to push up the sky,
imitate turtle, then butterfly.

Your mother, too, grieves by ritual,
cleans stove knobs with a toothpick,
stirs flour and butter into a roux.

Your father on the wooden floor
eases his quavering back
after radiation.

I refuse the vending machine's easy candy
to soothe the days: hours,
focus on training my future.

I incite night to swallow day quickly,
keep it from stretching like elastic
round and round, squeezing the heart.

Apocalypse

". . . and the earth and its works
will be burned up."

2 Peter 3:10

Morning awakens to voices of bird flutes
rising from meadowsweet, huckleberry,
combing through the coarse hair of nutsedge.

Squinting, you shield your eyes from the sting
of the sun as it charges uphill, the length
of a dirt road to a scrub-dried lawn.

Wild cherry, crepe myrtle, hydrangea droop,
annoyed that summer insists
holding off rain clouds, crumbling loam.

Wrens also can't agree if nesting in a sweetgum
is better than in the mouth
of a painted birdhouse.

Monarch butterflies, orange-yellow,
black-white pinioned, abandon their off-spring
on withering limbs of milkweed.

Nature is crawling, slithering, winging
its way poleward,
aiming to keep cool.

Your hope is the moon
chilling earth.

Listening

As day wipes perspiration off her forehead,
the evening star a rogue in the sky,
I listen to sourwood and sweetgum leaves.
They rustle and moan songs of an ancient sea
below, murmuring, steering millennia,
as if expatriates, through the valley.

Ignited by trappers one hundred years ago,
this foothill burned to the ground, invited
deciduous riff-raff that now climbs to the top,
brambles beneath scrappy fir. Trunks mottled gray,
limbs arthritic, trees cling to the seasons
at the whim of developers.

Possums, squirrels scatter as trails are hewn,
tracts dug into the hill to embrace dwellings.
Next summer youngsters will climb branches
and teens carve their first love inside a heart.
Trees will continue to shelter and shade,
hide sadness in their tangled underworld.

This evening they shake their heads and sigh.
I sigh with the trees. Time slowly closes the door.

Repainting the House

A swallowtail lights on purple salvia
open for a prod and sip
as I stroke pool water into a narrative of ribbons.
Crepe myrtle perfumes air,
sugars the green throats of hummingbirds.

Workers scrape blue blisters off house siding —
complaints that have festered from inside out.
My neck creaks as I stretch and bend muscles,
hoping to stop the settling of bones
that pinch with the decades.

Like a toad caught in my throat
sadness is unable to voice discontent.
It is difficult to give up any year with a swish of paint.

I spiral the corkscrew into Pinot Noir,
pop a whiff of bouquet into the kitchen,
smooth out anger with nectar.
Know I am one of many.

Like the ants colonizing our gray metal mailbox,
intersecting the mailman's delivery,
interpreting an alien alphabet.
They spill their black letters onto my hands and arms.
I brush them off,
dross on the pavement.

Tomorrow the workers will begin painting the house.
Same color, same trim.

III.

*"We weave our lives at times;
at times our lives are woven for us"*

—Bill Brown "Savor"

First Day of Fall

Morning drapes a cold shawl over your shoulders.
Rays still fondle spindly begonias,
flower brown-stemmed daisies.

Swallows zig-zag from tree to shrub,
flutter halos around feeders,
frenzy-feed on seeds.

You boil chicken, onion, and celery into a broth,
dice carrots and potatoes into squares,
dash nutmeg and salt into the swirl.

Gusts jostle and prod leaves
to loosen their grips,
forcing them into a final dance in air.

Rolls in the oven and soup's simmer
glide aromatic hands
up the spiral staircase to the ceiling.

Winter cowers behind Signal Mountain,
impatient to wrestle fall for a win.

Poetry of Scarves

for K.B.

Last night's wind swept leaves
in rainbow colors on the driveway
as a dust cloud draped
the city with a translucent scarf.

Inside the folds,
we hook our forefingers into cups,
sip tea at the *English Rose,*
browse through the heart's flood.

Inside the surge,
your burnished hair glows
against pumpkin and green weave.
Mine shines pale gold
ringed by violet and silver
like last night's hunter moon.

Inside the moon,
diaphanous silks shawl our throats
as we rise above
earth's dust and grit.

The Chimney Sweep

He listens to the swish of his broom
loosening wood tar, microbes
of creosote, singed bird feathers
softening brick. Thick layers deposited
by roaring fires of oak, hickory, sweet gum,
splintered wood clinging to the sides,
remains of our winter night arguments
channeling upward, finally erased.
He scours and scrapes the cavity
until his face is covered with soot,
the whites of his eyes gleaming
like two polished porcelain knobs.

The Closet

Aprons on hooks for my Cinderella hours
in this cathedral of apparel.
Silks hang mid-air like sermons,
sweatpants soft as the fur of our dog.

They wait for a daily litany:
under a cloud ceiling clothe me,
in drizzling rain shield me,
in eye-blinding sun color me.

In a corner a spider webs his narthex.
Summer shoes collect spores in pointed toes.
Cedar panels on wire hangers banish moths.

How years, like clothes, end up worn.
Wrinkles frown like unfulfilled prayers.
Loss pyramids the closet ledge.

I've learned to give up the mantle of love,
pets that died or ran away, daughters
growing their own lives.

Today, I air clothes on the backyard line,
let fresh apple scent of autumn
bead the rosaries of my days.

The Silk Road

Germans call it *Seidenstrasse*
pack animals once trekked
to silk the rest of the world.

I slip into my teal silk dress,
pair it with pearls,
little round moons
shining my throat.

Queen of fabrics
born of a white worm
devouring mulberry leaves,
spinning itself into a web of silk,

brought fortune
when Xilinshi dropped
a cocoon
into her afternoon tea.

Sheen glides over my body
like the moon's hands
over a still sea
at midnight.

Cruise on the Tennessee River

A vee of geese spears the sky.

A kingfisher darts into blue depth,
orange breast stippled yellow and rust,
the color of leaves.

Two bald eagles scale wind currents,
settle in the crowns of tall pines.
They remember the same aerie,
add a new alcove each year.

Ospreys gather for the flight south.

Milfoil creases the edge.
Cattails, bulrushes chamber the shore.

Hills glow as the sun pushes
waves toward dusk.

Day drowns distance.

Three Poets Read

for E. B.

Glasses perched on his nose tip
he sits by a quiet stream,
spills words slowly
into a narrow basin.
We watch them float by
on our matchbox boats.

Hair clutching her head,
she launches her lines
like missiles
that miss our minds by a fraction,
thud onto the wood floor.

Bold as a filbert,
hands edging the lectern,
this poet hooks his words to our hearts,
grabs our hands to dance with him,
or kiss romance
in the backseat of a Chevy
on a rain-soaked night.

The muse claims all of them,
dives deep to catch a school of fish,
picks words off orange blossoms.
But yesterday, last night at the poetry reading,
one poet's words walked by,
shook hands.

What He Harbors Inside Him

after Duty in Vietnam

His painting is a wall smeared
with roadkill, reds and browns
screaming for help.

When the muse strikes,
he strips off his shirt, re-paints,
and whips the entire wall
since only that day matters.

I see congealed blood,
spattered sobs in musty air.

Layers tell different selves
as he leads me to another wall
covered with burlap flaps.

He has started painting sackcloth
in panels, on the third layer.
He wants to paint what is unsaid,
wants me to lift
what is seen to soft speech,
dirge to melody.

Evening with Yo-Yo Ma

bow like a blade of grass
his encore strokes three voices
binds a spell

vibrato tender and sweet like a sip
of strawberry wine
or the wing
of an Adonis Blue brushing the cheek

the sun's fire rousing the day molto vivace
flickering in the clouds   between trees

until limbs release leaves largo
copper and carnelian
a slow giving of the season

finale a meteor shower
sparking the night
exploding on the tongue

bravo and bravissimo shower him
like seeds of cottonwood

All Souls Day

Morning red fringes the horizon's edge.

Last night snow twirled over the ridge,
sugar-coated fall flowers.

Nothing happens without God waving His hand.

A cardinal feasts on a spray of orange berries,
feathers green branches arcing the wall.

Wind tumbles leaves through the forest
like souls.

The beginning of mankind lives inside you.
The universe leans
where you give your time to the stars.

Serving Day at Channels of Love

"Not love,
not the wind,
not the inside of a stone" —Mary Oliver

After a lecture for the HIV-infected,
we slip on plastic gloves, smile,
ladle Taco soup into plastic bowls,
sprinkle shredded cheddar and chips
over the steaming broth.

Wafts blunt sharp edges of facts
gouging walls,
seeping into shoes,
cold as the inside of stones.

All night wind blew rain clouds,
opened faucets over bushes and trees.
The weakest leaves fall first,
others barely blush at the edges.

Leaving, acorn shells crunch our soles.

Study of *Pictured Rocks National Lakeshore, Michigan*

by Terry Donnelly

Mountains call me to cliffs and crags
stabbing the horizon,
not this lake rimmed in gold and brown leaves
against the blue, cloud-riddled sky,
ground dusted white,
telling of winter.

Reflected in the lake, the past
in a blur of trees, clouds,
my screen-sized glamor dreams.
No backbone to rein them in.
On the surface the years floating away,
sinking like leaves.

Riding future's horse,
I cling like a bird to the wind-furled mane,
strangely happy.

Carwash

At the corner of Main and Central, a white plastic chair
guards the front of the carwash.
Four in the afternoon traffic snails by
as if in line for a funeral procession.
The sun's shrill shine shivers the wind.

Like a good citizen, I sit and read the nation's headline:
Afghan Terrorists Attack. U.S. retaliates.

The carwash owner, Napoleon, wages his own Waterloo,
washes, rinses, and buffs
the worn metal and plastic shell,
the way God might cleanse and polish my soul.

Joe, his assistant, stands on a turned-over bucket
like a prophet to reach
neglected nooks for the sweep of the body.
Is this how I should measure up?

Cars come and go. Some stop at the crossroad,
wait for a light, a change.

History is a jewelry store up the street and on Gifford,
a half a mile from here, a new paint store.
Though the walls of our bedroom were primed three times,
the past years keep bleeding through.

Late afternoon musses my hair
as I watch others cope with what they were given.
I shift feet, glance up and down both streets,
tap fingertips over the nation's headline.
Easy is never a battle.

At the Art Deco Automobile Show

Nashville, TN

Bugatti, Jordan, Delahaye,
evoke an era of desire,
opulent symmetry spilling over us.
Hood ornaments the dot on an *i.*

The guide said, *Don't you know*
the designers must have loved women.

Our hands want to touch
curved fenders, fluid bodies,
hips, thighs, to glide fingers over
grille work as intricate as French lace.
Step onto broad running boards.

Don't touch.

Hands clasped behind our backs, we lean forward,
peek through almond-eyed windows
to supple leather interiors, malleable,
soft as the inside of a woman's hand.
Gauge instruments needle the dash,
buffed hand rails lure backseat passengers.

We imagine voluptuous half moons
hidden beneath silk shifts,
bead- and feather-jeweled.
Glitter gleams like glossed metal on cars.
The camera flashes into starbursts.

Fowl Love

Flannery O'Connor's childhood home, Savannah

I.

Day threads the sun's golden spindle
as your early years weave the parlor,
narrow hall and stairs, the front bedroom's
two windows facing *LaFayette Square.*

Masked by the screen of your "kiddiecoop"
you dreamed your first two years.
Warded off yellow fever.
Or holstered into a pram,
surveyed the Square like a Bantam rooster
counting hens each morning.

You cradled ruffled chickens like bonneted dolls,
insisted they nap in your "kiddiecoop."
Taught one of them to walk
backwards, as if pulled on a string.

II.

Huddled in the bathtub's cool porcelain
among feather pillows, you read *Grimm's Fairytales*
to your playmates. Between giggles,
you shared bites of poisoned apples
the witch offered,
out-ran the wolf roaming
the way to grandmother's house,
or in final desperation at the frog's gall,
threw him against the wall.

III.

Red climbers thorn backdoor steps.
Sun streaks through colored porch glass.
Clouds like mares' tails swish blue air.

Beneath the balmy scent of magnolia,
I look into your mirror, your love
for perversity and wishful thinking.

Betrayal

Deceit jingles his brain
like thirty used coins
as his demons wake

the stone of a kiss
wedged in his bones.
A fire blistering skin.

His mind a sea
drowning the sun's sequins,
shackling speech.

Gypsy moths
gnawed a path through flesh,
shredded his heart,

leaving it frayed
as wings
caught in hedge thorns.

Morning lifts
an arc of doves,
horizon lightening.

EXIT

Isenheim Altarpiece by Mathias Gruenewald

In 1512 he painted a life in panels,
their hinged doors open to death,
the last breath taken,
a Milky Way hulling the body
with its soft shell until it crumbles.

The last panel re-educates the body
with lance and spear, vinegar and sponge,
nerves spin spider nets of pain
over muscles, their four-ply threads rolled
into a ball, released as they elongate.

The mind shrinks from this thinking,
grits teeth, re-aligns eyes to the present:
Fall leaves grieve as they let go
the branch, the root.
Moans only the ground hears.
A dirge in gold and brown posed
against the sky's forgetfulness of light.
Each brush stroke a sigh for eternity.

Estate Sale

"This is not a place where you are not,
yet not a place where you are seen" —Rumi

A door-sized gold-framed mirror leans into a wall,
reflects the span of your life.

Crystal vases, bowls, wrought silver elephants shelved
like old friends, forgotten.

Chandelier earrings and precious stone necklaces wink
from a table, garnering light.

Testimony to a decade of confinement:
Crocheted squares sewn into tablecloths, bedspreads —
a wheelchair pushed into the corner.

Against the final years, days loop in and out
of windows, inviting dream worlds and stupor.

The sun's fingers prod each room for the soul not seen,
yet there.

In the Season of Grape Harvest

I.

In the season of grape harvest,
near frost and morning fog sweeten grapes.

Picking ripe berries first is an art
like knowing which word fits a poem perfectly.

Soil is the color of sandstone,
draws roots and juices
that echo through the vines.

A Lebanese dish of green beans, tomatoes,
onions, and spices flames your mouth
a swish of last year's wine cools.

Grapes plump and nectar our lives.

II.

In the season of grape harvest,
cumulus contrast, deepen the blue.

Wind lifts and scatters leaves
as I spread memory's bread with winter honey.

Longing for you is like a vineyard before harvest
seen through a window.

A taciturn sun hangs in thinning trees.

III.

Last night's frost cast a shimmering mist
over the fists of hydrangeas.

Inside an Egyptian tomb, a goddess
holds a cluster of grapes in her hands.

Vines require pruning, like a poem,
before tendrils curl along a strung wire.

In the kitchen, wafts of spicy red cabbage
remind me of your promises,
sweet as new wine.

IV.

I discovered that memory preserved
is like bottled wine I open.
If not stored properly,
it sours.

Second Life

—for Ursel

After raising three kids, she takes a brush,
dips it in blood red paint, rushes it over the canvas
from East to West, North to South, steps back.
She splashes drops of water like tears she shed
as her children grew into themselves,
watches the paint fracture and flow away.
She broaches grey and brown for shadows.
But that's the past. She slips a pencil brush in green
and gold, flecks grasses and wheat stands
across a field in Tennessee, heavy for harvest.
Her strong hands work quickly.
She spackles rose and plum, then curves
a blue helix of clouds for heaven,
a few smudges below,
smiles at the canvas that imitates chaos,
she, finally controlling her days,
unable to bleed past edges.
She backs away as colors cower or mesh,
then combs through a vision of children's hair,
dabs strands away with a fist of white cloth.
A rent of burlap in one corner reminds her
of the moments stolen swaying in a hammock,
a pinch of sand, then glitter strewn sparkles
the times she had to coax a smile.
She knows the light of morning slays
a long, dark night of waiting.
She trowels white pigment thinned with water,
a streak of lightning, a pool of light
in a backyard lake for luminosity and depth.
A few diffusing brush strokes before the final spray.
Children gone, she finds herself, her life,
a persevering heart.

Season of Falling

inspired by a quote by Oscar Wilde

This season knits and purls melancholy
on life's circular needle,
slips through my world's slanted door.
Birch leaves coin the walkway golden,
petunias spindle the garden wall,
roses splay petals, fall.

Knit one, yarn over, knit one.
A season for thinking, what if.
My mind zoom to Mars,
cold, barren peaks and craters,
rivulets left from a once huge ocean.
Microscopic life suspected
like our early beginnings.

Knit and purl, knit and purl, turn.
What if apocalyptic forces
follow a pattern
that will carve and splinter earth?

*Any place that we love
becomes our world.*

Wilde's words snap synapses.
Why leave this world for another?
Why disturb celestial designs?

Free will needles loops
of the unknown.
Don't drop one stitch —
it may unravel
an entire created work.

IV.

"There is a certain slant of light
on winter afternoons . . ."

—Emily Dickinson

"There are things you should know about snow
when it comes at night . . ."

—Bruce Majors "About Snow"

Im Steglitzer Stadtpark, Berlin

photograph by Barbara Schneider

Giant-trunked limbs lean in,
dome dark-dressed strollers
at the turn of the century.
They saunter in a shadowed network
afternoon sun throws
on white-dusted ground.

Roots murmur phrases of spring,
memorialize a green-splendored kingdom,
the bustle of birds and squirrels within.

The photographer savors stillness
in the realm of winter,
a sad let-go of light
at the end of the day,
but also a silent joy
in witnessing the season, the day,
this hour,
because it is yours.

Winter Scene

for Hemme

You must have looked up a thousand times,
easel splayed in this snowy meadow.
On white-washed canvas
you captured late afternoon light,
feathered a dusky-blue fir
and behind it a deciduous tree,
both casting blue-grey shadows.

I see your breath clouds,
egg-shell blue,
blowing warmth into your hands.

No children's sled gliding through snow,
no winter critters foraging ground.
The afternoon grown long.

Air white-blue and thinning,
you and I exist
in a watercolor winter.

Three Photographs of Goodness

I.

A calm sea sprinkled with floes
reminds of white lace covering pale skin.
Sun diffuses the sky
the color of a well-beaten egg.
Layers of fog doze in between.
White noise swing-dances with air.
Terns perch on the shore's railing.

II.

My dog sits in front of the cabin
next to a shovel leaning against the door.
He watches snow thrum mauve sky.
Ears pricked to the wind
blowing flakes sideways,
he listens to the faint call
of herding sheep in an ancient valley.

III.

In morning coat I saunter to the mailbox,
pick turbid news off the pavement.
Rain-doused winter trees scrubbed clean
branch morning birds whistling
their individual praise songs
as sun-drenched, light-blue air coaxes
a crusade of blooms early to the city.

Emily Dickinson Today

Dawn scrapes clouds for snow.
I lay aside the corset's bones,
wed my gossamer robe for the day.

His Kojak pate shines like a moon
into my morning face.
Words between us scatter like mice,
darting for a cranny.

I bite into a slice of day,
trickle over it a spoon of honey,
chew cinnamon toast slowly.

I always was in love
with my Farrah Fawcett wave,
the bouncy tickle on my ears,
similar to the sweet words
that once escaped your throat.

Books and TV lounge in our eyes,
handing hours to the clock.

Shadows write my thoughts on paper —
Are you nobody, too?
I died for beauty . . .
My night boots dusk over the ridge.

The Window

Leafless, tree limbs intersect
asphalt-gray sky like roads
while morning opens frosty shutters.
The valley still slumbers in fog.

Pansies in the window box cry for rain.
A chipmunk scuttles leaves for seeds.
One thing depends on another.
Fools face the world behind glass.

The Whole Picture

"I love you as certain dark things are to be loved,
in secret, between the shadow and the soul."
—Pablo Neruda *"100 Love Sonnets"*

Moon hikes over the horizon's ridge,
then frowns and trades luminescence
for striated shades of blue.
Stars balk but pledge
their return by evening, sending new light
like good neighbors.

Sipping coffee over the trifles of headlines,
a goldfish's memory spans three seconds,
an ostrich's eye is bigger than its brain,
I wonder what other news matters in my life,
if memory's love for you continues
or if reality out-runs imagination's sprint.

The sun staples hours
in her rotary album, pastes frowns, asides,
until I tire of the day's nagging voice,
the white noise love leaves behind.

Dusk veils thoughts.
Dew tempers winter trees
for another round of darkness,
moon throwing long shadows.

Three White Lilies by Georgia O'Keeffe

for Gerlinde

No doubt, the one leaning in is submissive,
perhaps kneeling . . .
Then why the need for one more,
a watcher standing outside
of marriage behind the two
who have lived together too long?

Look at this *menage a trois,* O'Keeffe's
apparent arrangement of disgrace.
Or is it grace that rains
through all seeds, grace that allows
a way to survive?

I used to smile at the moon's plump face
attuned to a night's symphony,
the arrangement of stars,
assured that a triangle's overt clang, clang
was useless to harmony.
I wonder if O'Keeffe knew, too,
a man's coiling, twisting claims of innocence
the way a woman soon learns to deny
the moon's phase within her.

Either way, she straightened herself
like a lily to the sun, half-smiled
at the day, allowed how she might as well
gather grief in her skirt
and place it to rest for the night
like a whiney child.

Who's to blame
if she's learned to keep herself
bound closely at the chest?

The Pedicurist

for Nikki

While snow clouds the sky,
she sits on her stool like a goddess
ruling over the underworld of feet,
toes splayed for submission.

She arms herself
with hook, file, clippers,
for the battle of soles,
ingrown toenails, wayward cuticles,
scrapes off callouses, corns, bunions.
She files hard
as if transgressions settled in feet,
crusted a ridge below the Achilles,
needing scouring like a pot.
She witnesses the silent fall
of flakes, marbling wood.

Her goddess hands palm and rub
life's currents
running in bursts through feet.
On and off switches the world pulls.

Soles newly innocent
as when leaving the creator's mind,
ready for the first imprint
in new snow.

What We Know

Winter trees spell loss
only coming seasons will restore.
Like us, branches are beggars
reaching for the morning sun.

Blood binds us in this forest
brushing wind and rain against the house.
You soap your body circular,
I in longitudes.

An array of shells, maps,
small trifles glorify our annual cruise,
mortgage paid off.

We ignore the owl's scorn,
raccoon scratching the glass door,
a coyote howling discontent.

The house bends and settles seasons.
Sometimes our dog answers the moon
staring into our curtain-less rooms.

Reunion on the Rhine River, Colmar — France

Our mouths are filled with words like death
as rain hangs deep and gray in clouds
and swans straddle swells at the river's edge.

Linden trees branch last night's friendship pledge,
those golden coins that fall on concrete loud,
now roll from our mouths again, forget death.

Our wishes for the next five-year reunion, a hedge
of wild grapevines growing in a narrow trough
aside swans straddling swells at the river's edge.

Anglers fish their lunch from the water's dredge.
Ferns and grasses play a dirge the waves shout
and our tongues imitate the notes of death.

One last embrace, a final *adieu* as distance fled
to the mountains veiled in fog. Listen to the sound
of swans straddling swells at the river's edge.

Past a field of yellow rape, rain and damp embed
our coats, hands in pockets full of doubt.
Our mouths empty and dry as when in death
swans straddle swells at the river's edge.

The Blue Door

In the end, his life a narrow blue door
framed in concrete posts,
opening only for leaving,
leaving on another military mission.

Five years in the jungles of Burma
returned him home to his wife and son
as stranger arguing
a half-empty glass of milk, full.

This door, this blue door
kicked in by memory today.
A year in Alaska,
then Louisiana to warm him again
for a conjugal meal.

He knew nothing of his wife's passion:
a crème-de-menthe at sundown,
her favorite books, the twang
of country music's romance.

Both knew the door's lock changed
with each assignment —
Pennsylvania, Kansas, Florida.
See the pin holes of regret,
the door's marred surface.

Calls and letters must have worn
and bent them,
like these faded boards.
Yet, they were bonded
for endurance.

In the end, his life a door shut.
This blue, blue door.

Bend in the Road

After the wake, the burial, the ocean
called us. For a week
we scanned the horizon for a revelation
as the waves pressed shoreward
into the remains of small lives.

What to do with an early dry sink,
two boudoir chairs, dishes
too fragile for every day, depression
glass stacked, linens yellowed,
two sea shells capturing
memory in a box.

Other years we collected conch, limpet,
and nautilus to display on the shelf
at home, beach-filled jars
for the garden path. This year
one grain, one shell is too much.
This year we begin traveling light.

Panacea

Winter sun pinches eyes
filled with the sea's graveyard —
histories laid bare.

Half spirals of life,
tiny beginnings,
each turn difficult,
striped with valor
or bare striations of deceit —
paths they had to go.

They lived the only way they knew
until they were done.

These remnants prick my soles,
send universal remedies
up my spine.

A boat sits at the horizon's edge,
fades in mist.

Incoming Sea

2002 watercolor on paper by Sally Miller

for Michael and Hannah

Love blindfolds reality,
dulls ears to the sound of sea
roiling against jagged rock
before it falls, expands, falls again.

Breakers collide, rumble,
like a train's steam engine
unable to stop.

Late shift over,
you propped your heads on rail,
wished your future on midnight stars,
woke in the next life.

Memory is a whistle's insistent blow,
a whirlpool of words inside me,
spume of white foam.
Ebb and flood.

Ocean drunk on water meshes blues,
chases two seagulls to clouds
like lost souls.

How long will the sky
blink messages at night?
How long before our beginnings end?

Sea and sky pour forth
what is written on our hearts.

Winter Storm

for Mama

The storm's center arrows north of us.
Clouds spindle ice into flakes,
dense stars.

Darkness and I sit in front of the fire.
Flames lunge at wood,
devour each splinter.

A storm lamp lights my page.
Childhood spells loneliness,
waiting for you to come home.

But at night, in our single bed,
you were mine
as the snow queen etched
dreams in window glass.

Things I Will Miss

for Everett

the long groan of the cupboard door
as I reach for the coffee tin
like a new day,
spoon darkness into the filter

reading the morning news with you,
our words circling the study,
repairing the net of family

my brain's small lamp switching on,
shedding its umbra over a new poem

the sun in March prying open
clasped buds of clematis
clutching cedar siding,
forcing roses rounding the pool

Tyler's four-paw trot home,
nosing the door open

toasting champagne with friends,
fizzle cribbling nose and feet,
my tongue oozing honey

your slight bend
as you stack logs for a fire,
striking the match

Star Waltz

When I have to die,
spread my ashes like seeds of goodwill
among Southern pine, sourwood, and sugar maple
guarding our house.
The trees know my scent after forty years
of hiking between or leaning against their trunks,
of calling and chasing the dog home.
They knew when the rattler hid beneath brush,
when the owl fluted my name
until morning.

Spread my ashes in a clearing of blood-red trillium,
in a bed of blue lady slippers
climbing a slope,
in the half circle of mountain laurels
opening their pink mouths
to scent the air.
Spread my ashes in the poison ivy patch
running along the ridge
for the moments I forgot my heart's home.

When I have to die,
spread me in the path of the raccoon, the hare,
the opossum, let their soft feet pad my ashes
to sponge litter and leaf mold,
so I can sink deep into earth and its fire,
the sign of my star.

Acknowledgements

The author would like to thank the following publications in which some of these poems were previously published:

Ekphrasis: Exit,
3Element Review: Second Life,
Abyss and Apex: Snow White in 2015,
Linden Avenue Literary Journal: Song,
One Trick Pony Review: When I let the River Answer, City Garden,
Quiddity: Bend in the Road,
Town Creek Poetry: Three Photographs of Goodness

Anthologies:

The Southern Poetry Anthology, Volume VI: Tennessee: Listening
Southern Light Anthology: Three White Lilies

• • •

The Closet and *Things I will miss* were inspired by Bill Brown's poetry and prompts

When I Let the River Answer was inspired by Marilyn Kallet's prompt, written at the banks of the Garonne in Auvillar, France

In the Season of Grape Harvest was written after reading Roseann Lloyd's poem *In the Season of Chanterrelles*

Fowl Love's "kiddiecoop" is built like a chicken coop with wood and wire mesh and a hinged top. The family used it to keep baby Flannery protected from mosquitoes.

In Appreciation:

The author would like to thank Diane Frank who encouraged this publication.

Thank you to K.B. Ballentine for her gentle advice and willingness to read drafts.

Thank you to the Thursday night poetry group for their help with revisions.

Thank you to Melanie Gendron for designing the cover and layout of this book.

Thank you to Earl Braggs and all poets and friends who encourage my writing.

A final thank you to Everett for his constant support and to Tyler who faithfully snoozes at my feet while the muse writes.

About the Author

Helga Kidder is a native of Germany's Black Forest region and lives in the Tennessee hills with her husband, Everett, and her dog, Tyler. She was awarded an MFA in Writing from Vermont College. She is co-founder of the Chattanooga Writers Guild and leads their poetry group. Her poetry most recently was featured in *Southern Light, Twelve Contemporary Southern Poets* and *The Southern Poetry Anthology: Tennessee*. She has participated in workshops in San Francisco and in Auvillar, France. She has two poetry collections, *Wild Plums (*2012 Finishing Line Press*)*, and *Luckier than the Stars (2013 Blue* Light Press).

Books by Helga Kidder

Wild Plums (2012) Finishing Line Press

Luckier than the Stars (2013) Blue Light Press